# ACROSS A DARK AND WILD SEA

WRITTEN AND ILLUSTRATED BY DON BROWN

CALLIGRAPHY BY DEBORAH NADEL

ROARING BROOK PRESS
BROOKFIELD, CONNECTICUT

Published by Roaring Brook Press

A division of The Millbrook Press, 2 Old New Milford Road, Brookfield, Connecticut 06804

Library of Congress Cataloging-in-Publication Data

Brown, Don, 1949—

Across a dark and wild sea / by Don Brown.

p.  cm.

1. Columba, Saint, 521–597—Juvenile literature.  2. Christian saints—Ireland—Biography—Juvenile literature.

[1. Columba, Saint, 521–597.  2. Saints.  3. Books and reading—History.]  I. Title.

BR1720.C623 B76 2002   270.2'092—dc21   [B]   2001019355


ISBN 0-7613-1534-9 (trade edition)   10  9  8  7  6  5  4  3  2  1

0-7613-2415-1 (library binding)   10  9  8  7  6  5  4  3  2  1


Printed in Hong Kong

First edition

*In loving memory of my mother, born Virginia Sheahan.*

*Daughter of Daniel Sheahan.*

*Granddaughter of Patrick Sheahan, of County Cork.*

# Columcille

WAS BORN IN 521.

HE WAS THE SON OF A KING, FROM A CORNER OF IRELAND SCRUBBED HARD BY OCEAN WINDS, IN A TIME THAT CAME TO BE KNOWN AS THE DARK AGES.

IT WAS THE DARKNESS OF IGNORANCE AND THE SHADOW IT CAST OVER PEOPLE'S MINDS.

For thousands of miles in every direction, armies marched and battles raged. The Roman Empire, which once sat atop the world of Columcille's ancestors, tottered and fell. And in its ruins lay knowledge and education. All of it—empire and culture—was swept away like yesterday's dust by new rulers.

Learning found no friend in them.

Books were destroyed or forgotten.

Reading and writing were like magic, and the people who knew their secrets as rare as wizards.

Columcille became one of them.

As a child, one story goes, Columcille was fed a cake filled with letters of the alphabet, and from that he came to love writing.

Still, it was at church schools that he learned how to shape letters, how to join letters to make words, and how to string words together into sentences. A person with this skill was called a scribe.

These schools were part of religious communities called monasteries, and were candles of learning in a dark world. Columcille became a monastery member known as a monk.

He also studied with an old bard, or poet. In the poems of the bards lay the history and stories of Ireland. Columcille learned them and wrote his own poems.

Prince, scribe, monk, bard. He was many things during a time when the accomplishment of even one thing would have been remarkable.

Columcille grew into a man, large and strong, who was devoted to the worthy life of a monk and bard. He tramped Ireland, established scores of monasteries, and wrote poems.

Large and strong, too, was his appetite for books. But there were few books, and his hunger was never satisfied.

During his travels, Columcille visited Finnian, who had been his monastery schoolmaster. He discovered that Finnian possessed a wonderful, beautiful book unlike any other in Ireland. It was a book of Bible psalms, or hymns, and came from the distant city of Rome. Columcille wished to make a copy, but was denied. Finnian was stubborn with the pride of owning the one-of-its-kind book.

Columcille was also stubborn. He secretly vowed to make a copy, and set himself to the task.

Like all books of the time, it would be a manuscript, which means "written by hand." There were no printing presses to make books, nor would there be for nearly 1,000 years.

Manuscripts were written with handmade pens and ink. The pens were cut from goose or swan quills. Ink was specially concocted according to its color. Black ink was made from soot, brown from oak apples and iron. One shade of blue came from a mineral brought from Afghanistan, and one red was made from an insect. Red was a favorite color, used to mark special occasions on the calendar. We still use the expression "red letter day" to mean an important or memorable day.

There was no paper, so scribes wrote on animal skin, stretched and scraped until it was so thin you could almost see through it. This was called parchment. Rectangular pages, called folios, were cut from the parchment.

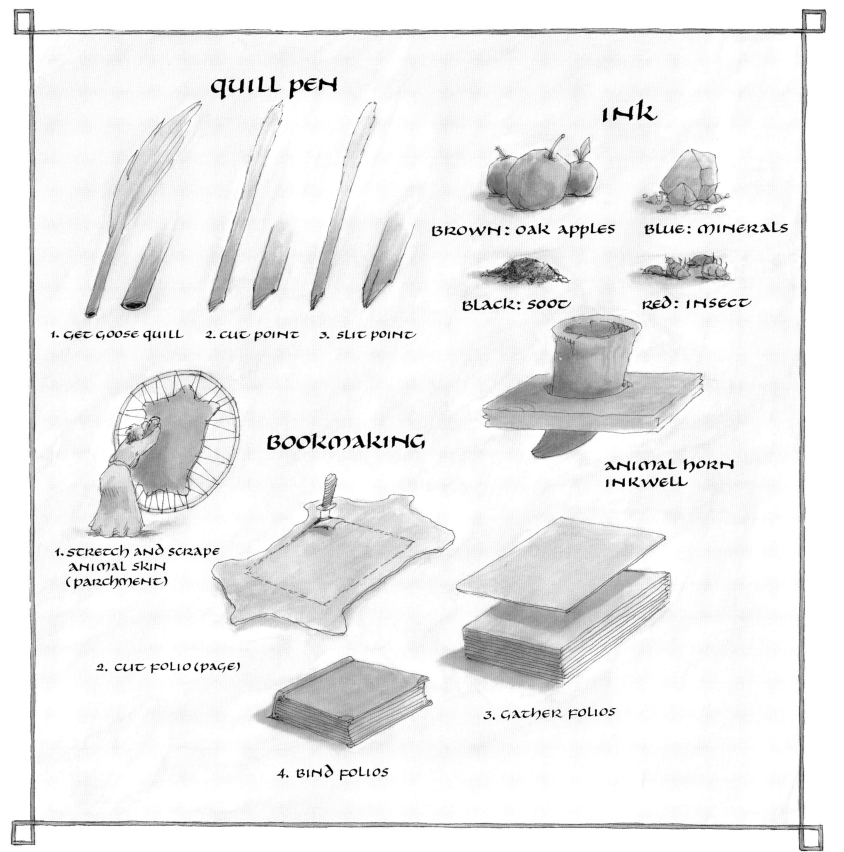

QUILL PEN

1. GET GOOSE QUILL    2. CUT POINT    3. SLIT POINT

INK

BROWN: OAK APPLES    BLUE: MINERALS

BLACK: SOOT    RED: INSECT

ANIMAL HORN INKWELL

BOOKMAKING

1. STRETCH AND SCRAPE ANIMAL SKIN (PARCHMENT)

2. CUT FOLIO (PAGE)

3. GATHER FOLIOS

4. BIND FOLIOS

Parchment, pens, and ink in hand, Columcille sneaked to Finnian's book at night when it was unguarded.

He laid flat the parchment, dipped quill into ink, and slowly copied. With strokes thick and thin, letters appeared. Clusters of letters became words. Teams of words made sentences. Parades of sentences filled pages.

Legend has it that as one hand wrote, the other one glowed and made light for Columcille to see.

After many nights—no one is certain exactly how many—the book was finished. But whatever joy Columcille might have felt was crushed by Finnian: News of the copy, as rare and desirable as a precious jewel, had spread, and Finnian demanded it!

Each man felt his own claim to the copy was true. Finnian argued that without the first book there could never have been a second, so surely both must be his. Columcille countered that the copy should be his, because he had made it. The argument swung back and forth, and tempers burned. Diarmait, the greatest king in Ireland, was called to decide.

The High King weighed Columcille's and Finnian's words and declared, "To every cow her calf, to every book its copy"—and awarded the book to Finnian.

Columcille was furious. His anger was a fever that took hold among his powerful friends and clan, or family. Diarmait, they argued, had no right to trifle with their kinsman, a learned monk and prince! Weapons were gathered and fighters rallied. They would punish the High King for his insulting judgment.

Followers of Columcille and Diarmait crashed together in a storm of swords and spears. At the battle's end, three thousand of Diarmait's fighters lay dead, but only one of Columcille's. The great king was defeated and the disputed book was recovered.

Yet the victory felt hollow and wrong to Columcille. The blood shed over the book had betrayed his pledge as a monk to live a worthy life. He decided he must be punished and set the punishment himself: He would leave his beloved Ireland to make a more worthy life elsewhere.

Columcille and twelve friends boarded a boat made of leather and set sail on a dark and wild sea.

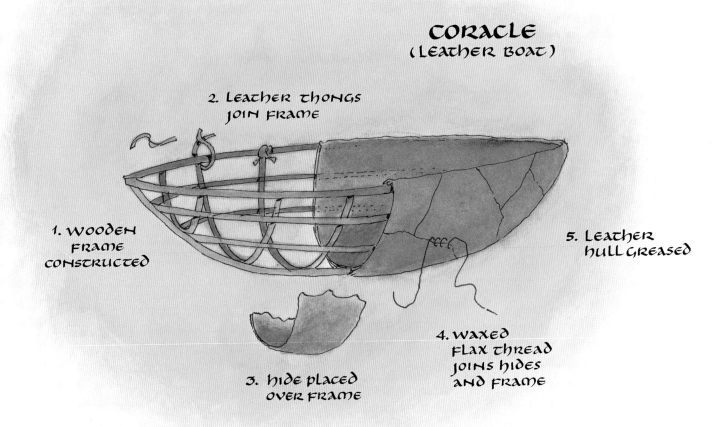

**CORACLE**
(LEATHER BOAT)

2. LEATHER THONGS JOIN FRAME

1. WOODEN FRAME CONSTRUCTED

5. LEATHER HULL GREASED

3. HIDE PLACED OVER FRAME

4. WAXED FLAX THREAD JOINS HIDES AND FRAME

They sailed until they could no longer see Ireland, to the rocky coast of Scotland and a tiny, empty island called Iona.

There they fashioned small, beehive-shaped shelters for each member of the group. They struggled to live worthy lives, and shared their faith with their Scottish neighbors. Inspired by their example, others joined them and, in time, a great monastery was built.

Columcille still loved books, and he still made copies. We can only guess that he found book owners who were more generous than Finnian. A building where books could be copied, called a scriptorium, was added to Iona. Scribes were nurtured and trained.

Books were made and dispatched, like small boats on a dark and wild sea, to places where reading and writing had been forgotten or ignored. The books made colonies of learning, and people's minds, once dark with ignorance, were brightened.

Columcille, the man who loved books, helped the world love books. So we remember him and retell his story.

# IN A BOOK

## Author's Note

Crimthann was born about 521 A.D. in northwest Ireland. He was born into one of the clans of pagan princes that then ruled Ireland, but he forsook his pagan heritage and the chance to become a king, perhaps even High King. Instead, he joined the church, and took the name Columcille (*koll*-m-kill) which means "Dove of the Churches."

Columcille was a pupil of Gemman, an old bard from Leinster, and studied at monastery schools, including one governed by Finnian. As a monk, he was devoted to his faith, and established monasteries at Derry (545), Durrow (553), and Kells (554); many other Irish monasteries claim him as their founder. Still, it appears that Columcille's roots remained strong. He is said to have enlisted his clan kinsmen in his dispute with Diarmait, the High King, over the ownership of a copy he had made of a Psalter (a book of Psalms) owned by Finnian. The clan, who chafed under the High King's rule, viewed Diarmait's ruling in favor of Finnian as another example of their oppression. A bloody battle followed at Culdremhne in 561, in which Diarmait was defeated and three thousand men died.

Columcille, perhaps dismayed by the ferocious bloodletting he fomented, departed Ireland about 563 and established a monastery in Iona, Scotland, on property likely provided by one of his pagan relatives. Much of his life was spent preaching to the Scots, known then as the Picts. (During his labors, Columcille traveled to Lock Ness and reportedly met its monster.) Western Scotland was almost entirely converted to Christianity by Columcille; for this, the faithful calls him a saint: St. Columba (Columba being the Latinized version of his name).

Columcille's Iona monastery flourished. Its scribes devoted themselves to bookmaking, as did monastery scribes all across Ireland and Scotland. Columcille himself is said to have transcribed more than three hundred books, and was working on a copy of a Psalter when he died in 597. Through the efforts of Columcille and others like him, the embers of literature and scholarship, nearly extinguished during the Dark Ages, were re-ignited. Remarkably, a few of the manuscripts from eighty generations ago are still with us. The Book of Kells, the Lindesfarne Gospels, and other mediaeval illuminated manuscripts are precious heirlooms of Western civilization. Even the book of Psalms that Columcille copied from Finnian, called *The Cathach of St. Columba*, survives and is part of the Royal Irish Academy collection in Dublin, Ireland. We treasure the manuscripts not only for their rare, stunning beauty, but also for the sentiment they embody: That words and ideas matter, and cherishing them is a labor of the ages.

The style of writing known as Uncial lettering appeared at the end of the Roman Empire and was widely used for Christian manuscripts through the Eighth Century. It consisted entirely of capital letters (right); lower case letters, or half uncials, were not employed until later.

# THE UNCIAL ALPHABET

## HAND LETTERING FROM
## THE TIME OF COLUMCILLE

## Bibliography

Adomnan of Iona, *Life of St. Columba*. Richard Sharpe, translator. New York: Penguin, 1995

Butler, Alban, *Butler's Lives of the Saints*. New York: P. J. Kenedy & Sons, c.1956

Cahill, Thomas, *How the Irish Saved Civilization*. New York: Doubleday, 1995

Foster, R. F., editor, *The Oxford Illustrated History of Ireland*. New York: Oxford University Press, 1989

Hartley, Dorothy, *Lost Country Life*. New York: Pantheon Books, c.1979

Meehan, Bernard, *The Book of Kells*. London: Thames and Hudson, 1994.

Weinstein, Krystyna, *The Art of Medieval Manuscripts*. San Diego: Laurel Glen Publishing, 1997.